PRETENTIOUS SLOBS

Lascivious Liberals Run in Mobs

by Karen Kellock Ph.D.

Manual for Superior Men

A complete theory based on Einstein physics, Political Psychology, Systems Theory and Archetypal Psychiatry.

FORMULA

**All success attraction
All disease obstruction
All recovery elimination**

You must fast on all three

OBSTRUCTIONS:

**People
Habit
Food**

PRETENTIOUS SLOBS

For no reason they turn against you in treason or build you up then hate you in your winning season.   You were down the ladder as a peon spat upon but now you're at the top, crowned.   Who imposed on you? Pretentious slobs that's who but it's only cuz you wanted their approval. They wanna believe the worst and fill their cup with it--they don't let you up easily or forget it.   It takes years to live something down so just relocate and start over in a happy home.

KNOW THYSELF

KNOW THYSELF

KNOW THYSELF AND FORGET THEM

Now that you know yourself--that what separates you is depth--you can just enjoy your life instead.

For either they're sick or influenced by someone who's sick: morally degraded from an era of lunatics.

Those who ask the most of you do the least for you. Remember that always/stay away too.

Pay them off, bid em well and thank God you're rid of em. They scammed you/go forth without em.

When they say they wanna help you then take your money and run Sue just block and learn too.

Because you were rebellious you had to build social muscle without us and it was hellish sis.

THE HERO'S PATH

They threw me to the wolves--they had to. I became a high wall separating me from everyone/all.

The chosen ones will suffer. That's the awful pain we had to go through to get to where we are.

The awful pain they put you thru caused you to step out in faith & that's the whole thing with God ok.

If you're a true chosen person of God expect persecution and then you'll make it son.

Being loved and cherished in this life does not indicate a chosen one. It's the opposite of that hon'.

PRETENTIOUS SLOBS

KAREN KELLOCK

KNOW THYSELF

When you got down they rejected you to your face so naturally you thought you were a nobody ok.

The devil knew your calling before you did. When you were in the womb he was planning for it.

Devil's plan: if he can get people to reject you enough you'll give up your destiny/reward from God.

God won't have you idol worshipping people cuz they will fail you every time with hidden evils.

SO THEY WANT YOU BACK

After spitting on you in the ditch, now you're up they wanna come back with a brand new pitch.

Now that God rescued and put you up they're coming around saying how much they love you, duh!

They threw you into the pit to suffer and lose your mind. No matter what you did you were bad, aye.

They treated you so bad they intended for you to never recover again. It toughened you, "friends".

One characteristic of the wicked is coming back as if nothing happened. See this and don't give in.

Smiling at your face with their fake ass energy acting like they're for you then turn to treachery.

While hating you they wanna take the place of God over you. Here's the contradiction making us blue.

LET THEM TALK

Let them talk, let family members continue to hate. They've been doing it so forget it all ok.

KNOW THYSELF

You weren't meant to fit in with those people who don't know God. This should relieve you a lot.

They don't know God cuz if they did they wouldn't treat you like that. Even momma became a rat.

Your haters gossiped about you constantly but God used that to elevate you far above honey.

What did you do to make them hate you? Nothing, they just wanted to. It's the default setting Sue.

Did they help you when suffering? When your family rejected you/said you were a nothing?

AFTER HEALING, WHY GO BACK?

After you endured all the crap they put you thru [and so strong too] why let em come in to renew?

Pay them off and bid them well. Tho' they scammed don't fight back cuz they'll take revenge Sue.

As a teacher your mindset is very broad so unless you attract the same the narrow see you as odd.

You never stay surface level and when you try it comes off as trouble. You have depth, doubled.

Pay em off and don't cause any trouble. You're better off to be rid of em with no revenge ya know.

ENABLING MOTHERS ARE A PROBLEM

Mothers justifying their kid's evil actions rather than standing up to them have demons in em.

These are evil influences from top to bottom and up again as all evil flows everywhere friends.

KNOW THYSELF

For this reason you gotta be a **PURITAN**--how America began: to separate from evil & keep it gone.

Now that you know yourself--that what separates you is depth--you can just enjoy your life instead.

Your fake friends never deserved you and you know it. You just settled for less to avoid loneliness.

If you need someone to keep you happy they will make you weak. To make progress knowledge is key.

Those who ask the most of you do the least for you. Remember that always to be happy.

ALL RECOVERY IS ELIMINATION

In pursuit of success what you eliminate from your life is just as important as what you add to it.

Your journey is unique. It's not a race against anyone else but you. Stop comparing and pursue.

A successful life requires you to take control where you can and eliminate time-wasters/bedlam.

Understand yourself and you won't seek approval from others. People-pleasing dilutes your power.

Notes of the hour: Seeking the vacillating approval of others means your giving away your power.

Resentment is like holding on to a hot coal to throw it at them. You're the one who gets burned then.

I'm for paying the scammers off, grateful they're outa your life and hopefully without any strife.

Go on, go on, go on knowing God'll get em. Revenge will hold you back & God does it better man.

KNOW THYSELF

Sin brings guilt and shame which is the basis of mental illness and all the toxic games in homes ok.

Sin makes em ugly: their beauty will droop. All temporary positives are quick to change too.

RESENTMENT IS POISON

Resentment poisons your spirit and saps your energy. It's a heavy chain tying you to dead past see.

Resentment diverts your focus from your aspirations. It's like a budget: your drive is going way down.

Chains to the past prevent opening a successful future. Knowing this helps to release it much better.

Forgiveness is efficient & selfish: a decision not to let the past ruin your mood or present success.

Mindless binge watching on Netflix or endless cycles of news: end this noise for the success cruise.

Create quiet spaces and times during the day. See the escape from noise essential for high-pay.

Dedicate time to reflection to weed thru all the noise and distractions. See this as essential son.

Even a few minutes of silence can up your mental clarity and reduce stress. Gratitude also does this.

PRIORITIZE PLEASE!

For success prioritize what really matters. What goals come first? Cut things that don't align sir.

You've avoided "doing nothing" but that is the most fertile ground for what you are wanting.

KNOW THYSELF

Beautiful So. California is now mostly drug infested and everywhere you look it assaults the senses.

A low startle response comes from trauma. I was like a cat in a room full of rocking chairs momma.

We have a right not to be misinformed. That means jail time for those on the fake media platforms.

If you don't trust God you'll call an old friend and swindler when you're in trouble: how odd.

POSITIVE AGING

I knew two men who suicided in their sixties to avoid old age. This is silly since it is the highest stage.

You're physically weaker and can't run a block, yes. But mentally you're a seer and superior/the best.

Having negative beliefs about age impacts your health even if subconsciously so be positive see.

The underlying stress may be conscious or not but it ruins our health as we see our aging as rot.

Having positive views of aging adds seven years to life. Seeing it negatively degrades you as you die.

Positive age beliefs protect you against hypertension, heart disease and cognitive decline my son.

The world is putting you down too as you grow older, compounding the problem til' you get hep sir.

AGE BEAUTIFULLY WITH DIGNITY

You can age beautifully/healthfully just by controlling aging beliefs despite these energy thieves.

KNOW THYSELF

Lest you see your aging as the apex of life--the crown of glory which it IS--you'll just decline & die.

Be a positive ager and hold onto beauty: you won't decline like peers but encourage youngsters.

Eat right and don't drink. Stay away from detractors or users and just continue on your journey see.

Wrong food or drink will kill an older person but if pure these latter days will be your best son.

Positive aging: It's not the end but the BEGINNING of the end--which is the best part my friend.

THEY FEAR TURNING THIRTY

I feared aging and turning thirty: all due to the messages I was getting from the male community.

In traditional societies the aged were giving first seat in the senate and were extremely respected.

Never view yourself thru "SMV": your sexual market value. That all goes down but it's all bull too.

Your true value is your WORTH: how God views you from what you've achieved/overcome first.

Perverted male community sees us as MEAT: SMV is about aging flesh not our divine spirit see.

AGE ACCEPTANCE IS ELATION

Once you really DO accept your age, it puts you in the present moment with gratitude for this stage.

You're not gonna put up with crap anymore cuz you don't have time. Every moment is sublime.

KNOW THYSELF

You can't have people around who provoke, you can't drink anymore nor smoke, it's just "OH!"

A Christian looks forward to going home again, to being with God in heaven--it's to a party we're goin'.

When mom died I realized my generation was next. One by one we're all gone: without God this sux.

Combined with this is the inability to relate to youth. It's like a different species and very scary too.

FROM THE BEGINNING GENERATIONS

From the beginning generations have come and gone so these feelings are experienced by everyone.

It's part of life: dying and death. But since we're wise at the end it can also inspire those who are left.

I don't wanna leave my home, pets & friends--making em more important approaching the end.

Every day is ultra-important to me now but when young the months and years slipped by in a fog.

I've never been more shrewd, refined or wizened and truthfully I've never looked better he's sayin'.

Would he/she have discarded someone they respected? Hell no they looked DOWN on you and rejected.

SAGACIOUS WISDOM IS HELL ON EM

These insights occur in old age and they're valuable as a sage so to youth you'll be ALL the rage.

You contain all the ages you ever were inside of you. That's a richness no earlier age has to view.

KNOW THYSELF

In my youth it was negativity and obsessive thinking but now I'm in control of thoughts and winning.

It should not be decline into death, but ascension to your highest then one day you die, that's it.

Thoughts, wrong decisions and people don't destroy your life anymore cuz you know the score.

If a man rests on his laurels he looks like Benjamin Franklin at 54--he's not cute anymore.

The Elect are blessed above all but they may not be able to have coffee, chocolate or alcohol.

MY CACAO JOURNEY

I respect the cacao--I draw lines. Just when I want more I put it away cuz it hits in 2 hours, aye.

Chocolate: For years I thought I was allergic but I refuse to accept this. I just drawn that line sis.

Chocolat: Don't panic, just enjoy it. It's a new ride and different but I think we can use it.

Racing heart doesn't mean heart attack but it does indicate sensitivity and need to cut back.

Once I get that first surge of elated energy I put the chocolate away because it surges all day.

A surge of racing elation: is this the chocolate ride I've been studyin'? I can't believe it's legal man.

They come wrapped in tiny pretty packages that are so power packed I recommend only half.

Chocolate makes me so high I can't believe it's legal! Cacao nourishes the mental/opens new windows.

KNOW THYSELF

Chocolatiers: Not only are we immensely enjoying the mornings we're also eating beauty food darling.

Chocolate: I avoided it for years cuz I had headaches at first but I pushed thru that--it's how it works.

No cacao after lunch. Put a cap on it with a salad or whatever cuz you're still affected til dinner.

Wolfe says cacao has off the charts nutrients so along with a salad why not stick to that friends?

Suggested salads after a.m. cacao session: Shrimp Louie, Greek/Chef's Salad or fish son.

My medicine turned to poison when I had more cacao in the afternoon. Vertigo, dizziness, nausea too.

Many stop the cacao in fear of colon cleansing. The laxative effect is real in all disease detoxing.

THEN THE TABLES TURNED...

All good things can be abused. Like never give your cacao to a dog or cat cuz it kills them too.

Cacao: should I use it, avoid it, restrict it, see it as dam addictive or quickly lose trust in it?

Maybe I don't want theobromine poisoning which is jittery nerves, racing heart or even worse.

I haven't felt myself since the cacao experiment. A little depressed which isn't like me said husband.

I'm a little leery now. These low carb dark chocolates are so strong I can't even believe they're legal.

I'll admit that mentally I'm more into things. But there's a fear in everything, an urgency, nerve endings.

KNOW THYSELF

The worse of theobromine poisoning is heart attack, think of that. Really, I'm praying about chocolat.

You add an Excedrin which has caffeine, doubling up like an amphetamine, and if also THC: deadly.

I am very sensitive to drugs and chemicals--cutting everything in half--and chocolate is scary stuff.

I wanna try it again, cuz I love the stuff, see if restriction helps--but my spirit says no more/that's all.

My spirit is afraid of the dark chocolate, there's a bad spirit in it for me now. Fear is not of God.

NOT EVEN A LICK AGAIN

I know chocolatiers who just suck on a piece and put it away, making it last all day. Maybe try that ok.

But just chewing and swallowing it like a candy bar? It's like taking a cannabis edible = hell on earth.

Heart racing and pounding outa your chest, wanting to call 911 from fear you're spinning too fast.

Just respect the dark chocolate, that's all I gotta say. Don't give it to cats or dogs & keep kids away.

The cacao effect lasts two days or more. The tail end is a downer so you wanna retake it as energizer.

It reminds me of alcohol withdrawal and "tail of the dog" which halts the terrible feelings in the fall.

I'm off the cacao & gave it all away. Even doing that made me leery, I see it as dangerous now see.

After an initial jolt it made me unhappy--I wasn't myself. It takes two days to get clear of this hell.

KNOW THYSELF

The 3 things that cause acid reflux with also heart palpitations are alcohol, coffee, chocolate!

Like all allergies it's addictive at first. I bought $300 of high end low carb chocolate, a total curse!

What it did to Ray's colon almost put him in the hospital and I've never been so scared as from cacao.

CHOCOLATE IS LIKE LUCIFER

Chocolate is like Lucifer: totally beautiful, smart or DELICIOUS but deadly in about 120 minutes.

You can't shake like that--as on a vibrator--and not fear heart attack. Coffee/cacao are BEANS Jack.

Fruitarians don't eat beans, thus they avoid peanuts. They eat nuts not this scary bean chocolate.

Beans make us NERVOUS cuz they're not right for us. Have all the coffee & cacao you want nuts.

It takes three days of suffering to get beans outa your system. One more day and I'll be free of em.

I was blessed with hypersensitivity but so easily this can turn on me if I don't watch what I eat.

The problem is the caffeine but it's inherent in the dark chocolate and it has a helluva lot.

BEANS ARE TOXIC PODS

Beans are toxic--pods collecting toxins from the rest of the plant. Coffee or cacao drives me mad.

So Freelee brought us bananas and Wolfe brought us toxic chocolate and and we all went for it.

KNOW THYSELF

Twelve more hours to full cacao withdrawal. I'm starting to feel like a happy child again y'all.

It may sound innocent but I had a bad experience with dark chocolate and son I'll never forget it.

I feel grateful to be alive today and have a renewed appreciation for just normal life/foods ok.

I lost control of my heart and nervous system, Ray his colon. Chocolate was the devil in our home.

That supercharged jolt of caffeine is not "happiness". That comes from normal living not madness.

END THOUGHTS

Politics is the intersection between incompetency and profligacy with other people's money.

They made permanent decisions on temporary emotions so let em stew, they made their bed son.

People go crazy when obsessed with their past sins while not realizing that they are forgiven.

PRETENTIOUS SLOBS

Lascivious Liberals Run in Mobs

LOTSA FRIENDS OR POWER
OH CINDERELLA
SELF-ABSORPTION AND ALCOHOLISM
NARCISSISM IS THE ABSENCE OF LOVE
EVIL ENEMIES
EXPERTS ON STUPID STUFF
IT'S ALL ABOUT SEX NOW
BROKEN BONDS LEAVE TRAUMA
THE MENTALLY ILL DON'T KNOW IT
FACEBOOK IS NOT REAL LIFE
ATTACHMENT DISORDERS
WE SEEK PROTECTION
WOMEN ARE INFERIOR THINKERS
INTROJECTIONS FROM BLOODY PAST
HIX POLITIX
FIGHTING TYRANNY IS OUR RESPONSIBILITY
IT'S ABOUT CONTROL AND <u>FORCE</u>
MUST KNOW WE'RE IN THE RIGHT
END THE NIGHTMARE OF THE SIXTIES
RECURRENTLY, FOX BASHES TRUMP
DEMOCRATS HATE LITTLE BABIES
TREASON GOES UNPUNISHED
TYRANNIES: TAXES, FINES AND FEES
PEDOPHILES WANT RIGHTS TOO
FEMINISTS LOVE BIG GOVERNMENT
TYRANTS AND PROCRASTINATORS
LASCIVIOUS LIBERALISM
SOAPS LURE WOMEN INTO NARRATIVE
THEIR ONLY RECOGNITION IS VICTIM-VALIDATION

PRETENTIOUS SLOBS

Lascivious Liberals Run in Mobs

THE DEAD VOTE DEMOCRAT, LITERALLY
THE SAVIOR OF AMERICA
JUST DESTROY THE OLD ORDER
HAVE FUN EXPOSING PEOPLE!
MEMORIALS OF PAST ARE USED TO BASH
IT'S WHITE REPLACEMENT
THE RIGHT TO DIS-ASSOCIATION
CAPITALISM BRINGS DOWN POVERTY
WEALTHY RACE HUSTLERS
MISERY CAMARADERIE
THE DIET OF FREEDOM!
DISCOVERIES DON'T TELL, THEY TRIGGER
GENIUS IS HELD DOWN BY *PEOPLE*
PROCRUSTEAN CONFORMITY
TRANSCEND HIX POLITIX
BE A SHINING EXEMPLAR
SOCIAL HYPNOTISM
BAD HABITS MAINTAIN BAD MEMORIES
PRIMITIVE GENIUS HAS MUCH TO OVERCOME
FORGET BLAME IF *YOU* LET EM IN!
GLOBAL BULLIES
YELLOW JACKETS ARE ABOUT INVASION
DAILY: DATES, SPUDS/RICE, MUSE/SLEEP
EVERYTHING'S COVERED IN FAT/SOY
LADYLIKE DATES NOT 1000 BANANAS
AUTHOR'S LAST WORDS
MUST GO 100% OR FORGET IT
BEAUTY WITHOUT SURGERY

Preface

LET THE PAST TEACH NOT ENCUMBER

Let the past teach you and wake you up about human nature but not weigh you down any more.

For no reason they turn against you in treason or build you up then hate you in a winning season.

Whatever they read about they'd pin on me. They made up stuff in one big smear campaign see.

Casting all cares on the Lord is key for me. For shame or guilt ask Him to share it and you're free.

You're were down the ladder as a peon looked down upon but now you're at the top, crowned.

Who imposed on you? Pretentious slobs that's who. But it's only cuz you wanted their approval.

The daughter of a raging scrapping brawling drunken mother becomes neurotic--no mystery there

So it is not mean to walk away and tell your story giving immediate relief to other victims of treachery.

PEOPLE PROBLEMS AND TERROR

It's unimaginable terror being thrown at the mercy of people who don't want you and no cops too.

If the law protects you you're lucky but the Jews faced the mob unprotected from cruel treachery.

Did you mother protect you from your sister or from the daddy lecher? It's a pivotal point for sure.

Preface to PRETENTIOUS SLOBS

Once it was clear cops wouldn't step in the kids went to war with absolutely no repercussions.

I got used to being unprotected--never expecting any--and their disbelief that it wasn't my fault really.

It takes years to live something down so why not just relocate and start all over in a happy home?

NAZI GERMANY COMPARISONS

They wanna believe the worst and fill their cup with it. They don't let you up that easily or forget it.

They broke my windows/killed my dog and cops wouldn't do anything. The Nazis of Borrego Springs

Jews in Nazi Germany: of course it's a false comparison but the dynamics are the same ma'am.

Gangs of ordinary boys would strip the women and chase them around the block throwing rocks.

There's a side to human nature when unleashed is terrible even in those you normally respect sir.

A beautiful home in a safe place is the greatest achievement in life. I'll be here until I die.

From the left brain we zero in on his faults. From the right we see the whole/all he does for us.

THE BEST IS BEING HELD BACK

Here you're the best but you're held back by guilt or shame in the past. Share this with Jesus.

I was rebelling against mom's personality. As soon as I'd concentrate or study she'd interrupt me.

Preface to PRETENTIOUS SLOBS

Later men would be jealous of my nose in a book. Privacy was something I could just never get.

They peg your differences with evil labels and projections, seeing their error only later on.

I always felt sidelined out, "let me in". It was pitiful until I saw the matrix of liberal vs. conservative.

It was my view of the world being attacked at every turn. I was just too different, they couldn't discern.

If you feel embarrassed to be alive give it to Jesus cuz it was for your high end superiority He died.

If scared of impending doom share that with Him too. You should feel happy and safe soon.

BATTLEFIELD IN THE MIND

The battlefield of the mind is the devil influencing our moods by these negative inner feuds.

The intrusive thoughts marking PTSD is the devil inputing his dam influence ruining the day.

God wants you to be King or Queen of your own domain not to be held back by guilt and shame.

Share it with Him as if you're yoked together. Let all those troubles go to the other side forever.

The burden of guilt/shame is horrible and heavy. It's a brick to carry not a catalyst for destiny.

You can be happy and creative then "it" pops into your mind ruining the day and everything you did.

Let Him take on your ugly thoughts about yourself while you stay what He wants, His magic elf.

Preface to PRETENTIOUS SLOBS

Why go to all the trouble of relocating if you're still back there in your mind? Forget that era/go blind.

Most holocaust survivors never think of any of it again. Use that as a lesson and forget it all then.

THEY PERSECUTE IN CONTEXT

The Jew was disdained and given a number but after the war had to regain self-esteem/be clever.

It's the **CONTEXT** that defines us so going no contact or relocating is key to reinventing an identity.

Suddenly your adaptations are different, the mal-adaptations disperse and you're clear not dense.

I was traumatized in my twenties. I lost both parents suddenly and my husband became an alki.

For years I walked around a nameless faceless lost creature then built up slowly with the Master.

THE WORLD THAT WAS

It was the ontologically fatal insight that the world was not what I thought it was/I was confused.

I became a walking bull's eye, a target with a magnet to anyone attracted, a succession of dirty rats.

Every negative emotion that comes up, share with Jesus. Get in that habit to be free of this.

God saved me from the human mess and then put me in a tiny cabin in the desert wilderness.

There for 26 years I was on the Potter's wheel and it was like a giant test: how deep can I feel?

Preface to PRETENTIOUS SLOBS

Fights: instead of running into the arms of another man run to God for He's got a much better plan.

If they're already all against you and you get drunk to cope your end is near as they get a rope.

"Bless and release" puts us back as CEO of our lives. To get past the dark trauma of secrecy/lies.

TRAUMA KEEPS SCORE IN BODY

What we're feeling is from past experience: trauma doesn't disappear, it remains locked in us.

It's not a death sentence, there's a silver lining of tapping into our higher self which saves us.

Being berated, trapped and scapegoated by a family mob releases wisdom we would not have.

It may hurt to lose a family but look at the bigger picture: do you wanna stay and be tortured?

Do you want to continue a relationship with a bully, an emotional vampire, a drainer of joy, really?

Loss in this case turns out to be a positive gain making you the Ace. Jesus came to divide, ok?

It may seem cold to say that people live/die, come and go but they're temporal, only God is eternal.

DON'T FEEL GUILTY FOR SEPARATION

Many scapegoats manage to get out but feel guilty for leaving their whole life--this is wasteful, no?

When thinking of em makes you anxious there's dysfunction and it's best saying good riddance.

The old miserable life of being trapped with my false accusers is over and now I'm on top sir.

Preface to PRETENTIOUS SLOBS

False accusation: inner conflict and stomach problems. Being silenced: throat maladies and choking.

The body keeps score though you think the trauma's over. Also, less audacity/boldness/clever.

I was a zombie, I had lost my tongue, I had no identity and was aging quickly, no longer young.

They supported my enemies tho' they didn't even know em. Anything to get to me, my family of origin.

BEING SILENCED AND CHOKING

I stopped eating cuz i'd only choke in my sleep. One problem creates another adapting to peeps.

Ragaholic mother was protected in home but copycat daughter was punished out there alone.

No one can take from you your healthy strong boundaries now or your story of the family mob.

For there are many who were pushed around and squashed like that, projections of dirty rats.

There were many squashed by female bullies, far worse and more sadistic than men see.

Mother's always pissed off having bought a lie, daughter copies that getting worse until she dies.

She looks like such a nice girl, a nice lady, a wholesome older woman--but inside they're scorpions.

Get past looks or social image cuz its got nothing to do with the inner man/woman doing damage.

I don.'t care what anyone thinks, that's maturity. You want em all to think like you, that's tyranny.

PRETENTIOUS SLOBS

Lascivious Liberals Run in Mobs

LOTSA FRIENDS OR POWER

I had to go thru all that to know what it's like to be controlled, eclipsed, to lose liberty.

A traumatized female may run to males for protection and that means sex: wrong direction.

The realization that we have no friends is freeing so now nothing smudges God's design, amen.

Less friends, more power. Give up illusions they protect you: God protects his children every hour.

People come and go, they are impermanent. God is eternal, He's there for the repentant.

Give up on brainwashed friends by CNN and in comes a flow of patriots and lovers of truth, amen!

Don't keep fighting past lowlifes in mind--what you shoulda said! It drags you down instead.

To be a good leader you must understand immaturity for it's everywhere, even in old men/ladies.

Most women are inferior thinkers: they're democrats who believe in abortion up to birth--and after.

OH CINDERELLA

Locked into two sisters who hate you becomes a traumatized personality. In these painful prison wee maladapt see.

Triangulation: locked into two sisters who hate you is hell on earth, you can't escape the curse.

PRETENTIOUS SLOBS

Having two sisters JEALOUS of her was war under the same roof, no wonder she's so aloof.

It's hard coming to terms with where there was lovebombing it wasn't a relationship, but accept it.

Narcissists like to generate flying monkeys who are on their team and who will confront you see.

SELF-ABSORPTION AND ALCOHOLISM

Self-absorption plus passive-aggression means relationship collapse from not caring.

Alcoholism indicates full on self-absorption and that means you don't really care if they're fallin'

When he resumed his drinking career I couldn't believe how he didn't care about what we shared.

Alcoholism is one of the ways narcissists show they don't do life well, they'd rather sink in swill.

All he knows is bourbon makes him feel good and you object so to hell with you, understood?

It becomes too irksome so bourbon is their only friend, committed to their own self-absorption.

Narcissism can be defined as the absence of love. So can they love? The answer is no dove.

He was Jolly Jimmy to the world but scornful and rejecting to his wife behind closed doors.

NARCISSISM IS THE ABSENCE OF LOVE

He may like infatuation or loves being in love but it's utilitarian, not there through thick and thin.

PRETENTIOUS SLOBS

Does this extend to pets? Unfortunately it does, when no longer utile they're cold as it gets.

Working our differences to allow collaboration and mutuality is not there: it's all about them.

They'll portray themselves in a loving way but it's all about them so it's only fake/temporary.

If family/friends are narcissistic you feel no one in the world understands and you feel sick.

Lord, I feel so all alone in my circle. I guess the whole world is like this but I'm so miserable.

Mature way of life: goodness & decency. Narcissistic self-absorption: I couldn't care less honey.

Go into solitude to calibrate who you are and why you do what you do: that's the solution dear.

EVIL ENEMIES

I watched as she killed her husband. First by giving him margarine then by killing his patriot visions.

The evil enemy lives a long long life. This is God's consolation cuz he's going to hell, bye.

Never fret when foe flourishes like the olive tree for he'll be cut down in the morning, wait and see.

If the angry liberal mob doesn't get it's way there's a price to pay. Look out: move, stay away.

Left's always on offense, not caring if your freedom's at stake: they wanna destroy you and fast.

You're cisgender, I'm female but it doesn't matter. Refuse these pronouns non-existing prior.

PRETENTIOUS SLOBS

They are political activists disguised as journalists. They are rabble rousers, we can see this.

EXPERTS ON STUPID STUFF

The average person isn't dumb just an expert on stupid stuff--the artificial reality of TV fluff.

It's the Dunning-Kruger Effect of the dumb thinking they're smart having moral virtue about this, or that.

If you treat someone like a celebrity they'll treat you like a fan or even worse, a servant sycophant.

To escape noxious influences of people past and present, get into the ELEMENTS--you'll love em.

The sound of the crickets at night, the afternoon breeze or the crows in the morning erases depression.

The devil in you is triggering early trauma bonds so I'm going no-contact to return to the elements/home.

As exhilarating/exciting as it would be I just have to bow out cuz it's [a demon?] too intense for me, see?

Anything so alluring wrecks self-respect and decency--it's of the devil as it begs "come and join me".

We the people did not buy their garbage. That era is dead--now we have risen up, refurbished.

IT'S ALL ABOUT SEX **NOW**

He's actually bragging he's had 10,000 women but he's a shameless, dirty/filthy sinner to a Christian.

His talk about all the sex he's had with women predictably triggers desire in his female fanbase of vermin.

PRETENTIOUS SLOBS

But his sexual braggadocio turns off the good ones who escape his echo chamber of who-you-knows.

He thinks being a whoremonger is a feather in his cap. Sexual Market Value [SMV] makes him think that.

No-contact includes all his friends. Let's say you don't see him but talk to them then you're hooked back in.

It's who you are to God: How can a new man respect you if he sees you disrespected your previous vows?

The perfect and most wonderful husband needs your marriage like he needs air, a soulmate pair.

The most perfect husband sees you and no one else. God brought you together and nothing's by chance.

The inferior man sees no soul mate/you're dispensable. He doesn't need you and it's not just you ya' know.

BROKEN BONDS LEAVE TRAUMA

It was a 30 year psychological WAR based on a broken trauma bond with the maternal element, mom.

When I forgave mom it all came together like a jigsaw puzzle where it had been chaos and bedlam.

No more hot desert climates for me, where I live in fear of the AC going off or an outage. I enjoy mild.

Just as God promises perseverance for us we must ensure it for our pets: be with em to the end, please!

For all the lovingness of the lovelies liberals created cruel, viscious, coldblooded independent movies.

Liberals are IMPOSING. They impose their ruthless rules, narratives and worldviews blocking the muse.

PRETENTIOUS SLOBS

Being Scotch and German I'm very into having a method for everything, exactitude and analyzing.

The deleterious effects of living in a land without justice where no matter what they get away with it.

Letting criminals go/not arresting: this is anarchy and the communist/big donors are behind it believe me.

Not arresting teen thugs vandalizing homes was happening in the 80's and it's ten times worse today.

It's Worthy Debate v.s. the liberal device of shutting you down cuz they don't like what you say.

THE MENTALLY ILL DON'T KNOW IT

Mental Illness occurs when you don't know you have it or how to relieve it-- only in retrospect do you see it.

You thought you were crazy/outa control but now you see it was just a SYNDROME and totally predictable.

It was very humiliating when they threw paper airplanes at me and I shut down due to hypersesnsitivity.

We can't stand seeing mediocrity get so much adulation but that's the situation in an imploding nation.

They could never socialize me no matter what they did. I adapted thru silence, smiling or tilting my head.

It's science or silence. No more games, small talk/trivia but speaking truth no matter what/taking chances.

It's disappointing to see your dispensability/lowness on the totem pole but greatly beneficial for y'all.

And women: you were always the initiator and women should not chase men. STOP this now, repent.

PRETENTIOUS SLOBS

FACEBOOK IS NOT REAL LIFE

I finally figured out facebook was not real life. It's my immediate surroundings where meaning is rife.

When we leave this world it has no more bearing and we won't even remember it. Think of that/reject it.

The transitoriness of events is enough to show we're wasting our time--especially as elders, oh my.

Memories are bad if you're viewing history with you as victim--it forms a template of humiliation.

See who your tormenters are today--weaklings with no say--not back then when they bullied their prey.

Overcome Momma's Spirit and return to the Father--now you'll be able to confront it when you see it.

Trump pays the U.S. Treasury and the Chinese pay Hunter Biden but the progressives still all love him.

Whenever you see women taking over you know the world is coming to an end. Jesse Lee Peterson

What is "momma's spirit"? An ornery, self-justifying, liberal, virtue-signaling, blame-shifting feminist.

I ate wrong on Friday: I cheated. I was sick/ravaged in gut pain until Monday, the whole weekend wasted.

Fat and soy dumbs us down--they've everything to gain by keeping us confused/belittled with face so round.

Take a look at people in the fifties and compare them to today. It's like a totally different species, ok?

People had decency/class and there was no gross. Higher thinking in thin waists and elongated faces.

PRETENTIOUS SLOBS

You're obviously racist--that's their answer for everything. You can't explain how they're wrong/creating misery.

ATTACHMENT DISORDERS

All addiction stems from attachment disorders, but unmet childhood development needs aren't forever.

They grew up in families where parents are shut down emotionally--no guidelines on what to do or say.

When the parents are drunk, passed out or carousing it leaves us with an ACHE in the gut, forsaken.

Unmet needs are an itch for which there's no scratch but addiction to alcohol/drugs/people are the result.

When clients heal from loving their rejector it's explosive and joyfilled after a life of misery, failure, nil.

After age seven there's no one on earth who can fill that need. You must do it yourself, then you're free.

The prevalence of alcoholism/narcissism means the parents aren't present for the next generation.

You can't just BE, your mind is always on the run because it's too painful to just sit and enjoy the sun.

Can't face the vastness of rejection/coldness so the mind gets ATTACHED to things to blunt the mess.

WE SEEK PROTECTION

We're running to something that will feed us and keep us safe but unfortunately it's a treacherous mate.

We search for external things to numb us to the ache. We simultaneously go into denial about it/we fake.

PRETENTIOUS SLOBS

Addiction means we zero in on it to the exclusion of everything else and terrible mistakes result.

So it's all about looks & youth and not about brains, how unfortunate for the human race.

The minute I'd slow down it'd all come back: the rejection, the slight, the theft and these were all facts.

Block it out, compartmentalize it, do anything to not FEEL it--again and again, there's never an end to it.

As a youth I'd drink to block it out. That didn't work so later it was assiduity/rigid routines while still a nut.

I knew MANY liberal women and none remain, no not one. They hate my guts for loving President Trump.

WOMEN ARE INFERIOR THINKERS

They just can't think, they're inferior thinkers. That's a statistical fact: women conform to each other.

He doesn't help me that way. He makes it possible for me to do it on my own by keeping the herd away.

He doesn't tell me how beautiful I am or how much he loves me. He enables the rollout of my destiny.

One frenemy mimicked a nervous breakdown at my loving Trump. These women are insane I thunk.

When my sister rallied for Pocahontas and the Bernie Communist I saw who she was, a liberal scuz.

I hear people yelling at me. Does it mean I'm schizophrenic or did I just swallow an introject of thee?

She was a nice enough lady but had liberal notions she imposed on me and that was our ending.

PRETENTIOUS SLOBS

He's turned a home into a trailer/parking lot while degrading into mediocrity cuza all the people around.

It's attachment to [often weird] people and making them king cuza you're own childhood neglecting.

You think you're the only one with autonomisms--uncontrollable things said/done? No way hon'

Since we're to be "all one", no disagreement is allowed as far as doctrine-- THIS is the end of the Christian.

Because Trump's the greatest: Some of us can think and reason, impervious to social hypnotism.

Biden failed to fire up his base AND he failed at changing minds of undecidants: now we're optimists.

INTROJECTIONS FROM BLOODY PAST

I can hear people yelling at me. Must be schizophrenia or is it just memory? Mom was persistent you see.

Women: You should want a man who needs you like water and sees you as his soulmate and none other.

People have no respect for your privacy since they've adapted socially. They MUST be taught, immediately.

They will bring their [unvetted] friends over, they'll overstay, they'll come unannounced, ok?

Their lives are so empty they need YOU to fill em out--the more you seek privacy the more they'll pout.

Every time in 30 years someone came over I felt imposed on. Every time! It's a social-cultural invasion.

Especially when someone came into my little cabin, I felt my abode go into a black cloud/I feared em.

PRETENTIOUS SLOBS

People are too close, too chummy, kissy/huggy yet a frenemy as you'll see in your future honey.

HIX POLITIX

We don't want em here. They've taken jobs from the citizens and won't adapt to us/the first tiers.

We love Trump cuz he's the greatest. Some of us can think and reason, impervious to social hypnotism.

The democrats have become the party of abortion. Think of that: they don't care about unborn children.

Paradoxically it's idiocy that displays itself as moral virtue and we see it every day in a person next to you.

Filling a vacancy isn't "stacking the court". To do battle we gotta push back every lie of this sort.

TDS is implicit bias. From men it's jealousy/from women it's fear of [strong male] patriarchy--all bull to you and me.

MOST academics are liberals and they all have TDS: they really don't know why they hate Trump's guts.

Chris Wallace spent the whole debate yelling at Trump, who nonetheless floored them all cuz he's top.

Slaves had to wear masks, only the politicians could be seen. This has always been the goal, ya' think?

Trump's getting covid has completely changed the climate--we're gonna have to wear masks forever man.

FIGHTING TYRANNY IS OUR RESPONSIBILITY

It's our responsibility to fight this tyranny. What they call "tolerance" is really waging war on stability.

PRETENTIOUS SLOBS

The Animating Contest: is becoming your best through fighting for liberty (your own and for me).

The Founding Fathers were all about defending freedom against tyranny, with guns mostly.

The only thing standing between us and total tyranny is an armed citizenry--that means you and me.

San Diego is so beautiful. But, the grid's gonna go down with gang activity all around.

Liberals don't care about people, only their vision of how things should be and that's why we're unfree.

Just when we need our weapons the most he sought to take them away? Americans felt betrayed.

Tyranny always masks itself--trying to "comfort": Those false words and propaganda from Obummer.

There should be no more envy/competition between us. freedom is all we want, so let's discuss.

Just when invaders wanna kill us he wants to take our guns? With leftists we should be done!

The irony is it's the left which is violent. Like liberals in families who shun patriots with silence.

Liberal psychologists call you mentally ill and then take your guns. This is trouble: tons.

If you protect yourself you'll be a minority of one--everyone is stuck in normalcy bias--but you must.

IT'S ABOUT CONTROL AND <u>FORCE</u>

It's about control--forcing them to see therapists if they dare disagree: This is tyranny.

PRETENTIOUS SLOBS

Oneism is false doctrine sending you to hell. Twoism is divine relationship with your father, a male.

Deceitful assumptions of virtue: they are not what they appear to be.

You're not gods and goddesses. You're sinners so get offa this.

Watch as liberal feminists rat out their ex-es. They love to label and diagnose men as the sexists.

The Bill of Rights doesn't apply if you're white, male and Christian. Imagine that: take it in.

For those with Sanders- or Hillary-lovers in your family: See the gravity and how embarrassing, chilling.

Tyrants target classes of people and that's why it is so serious as we're overcome with evil.

Imploding societies demonstrate an explosion of homosexuality--not judging, it's reality.

Liberals refuse to recognize cycles in history--to them everything is always the same. Lame.

They've wanted to take the guns from the sixties and now they're in control: the old hippies.

Liberals are evil people. They're committed to sin and run in packs to kill, destroy and steal.

To liberals this is Obama's stealth: Let violent immigrants in then destroy our right to defend ourselves.

The worst police tyranny is killing your dog just cuz they felt like it--it's how SWAT teams do it.

MUST KNOW WE'RE IN THE RIGHT

The one thing to know is we are in the right. Right always wins, doesn't it? Now good night.

PRETENTIOUS SLOBS

This isn't what we want--these elites furnished by globalists, creating wars and lying to all of us.

Evil liberals have been dismantling this country for decades. It's the world of the dead: Hades.

Here's another one for those who don't know what's going on: We're goin' down, down, down.

You mean to tell me all my parent's friends happily married 50 years were actually "gay"? Yah, ok.

People are attracted to it because they're in the majority. That's liberalism-- it's just polls, really.

GET A BIGGER SWORD

If foe has an AR15 you need an AR15, obviously. Jesus said it about the Roman sword--get a better one, ok

The left wins whether republicans are in there or not. All through gov it's theft, backroom deals and rot.

No fly lists: If you're on the list the Nazis they say you can't travel--you're goin' to the ghetto.

Bringing in radicals to attack us then taking our rights when we DO get attacked: tyranny facts.

The only solution to gangster government is open carry nation-wide. Pass laws or moral slide.

You collaborators who went along with this: You destroyed your future too by thinking he was cool.

Taking our guns, saying our kids belong to them, teaching us how to talk: the level makes me balk.

You don't even get the power but now you're supposed to go along with this and love it!

PRETENTIOUS SLOBS

Soros, Obama, Hillary, Moore and all you other trash. We will not submit, expect backlash.

END THE NIGHTMARE OF THE SIXTIES

We need to end this nightmare era starting in the sixties. These dinosaurs need to die out, truly.

Slaves don't have free speech and slaves can't own guns. They're totally vulnerable--no fun.

Obama's attempt to overthrow the country, aided and abetted by congress: These are facts, not guess.

You have no idea the pressure I was under having to adapt to liberals. It stinks what they think.

Scenario: 1. Trump surges. 2. Obama is threatened. 3. False flag. 4. Martial Law declared. 5. Guns taken.

The Right to Bear Arms came intertwined with individual liberty. Anything else is Tyranny.

Tyranny is terrible as they decide to cast whole groups in a net. Suddenly it's worse to be a vet.

It's scary living in a dumbed down generation without vision and who only vote by name recognition.

Let me get this straight. He wouldn't fight ISIS, brought them here while taking our guns: of course we feared.

America wasn't perfect but at least we had ideals. That made us unique: freedom is the appeal.

RECURRENTLY, FOX BASHES TRUMP

FOX is bashing Trump! Reason enough to drop them cold, they're boring and will end in a slump.

PRETENTIOUS SLOBS

The globalists raise taxes and exempt themselves. Then they take the guns cuz tyranny never stops.

Obamagration: Flooding our cities with criminals and Jihadists and these people were sadists!

The evil democrats lost and will never get in again! Trump was surging with the greatest win!

Every department has SWAT teams. They break in at midnight, kill dogs and wreck your dreams.

Because they're cowards dems target the innocent--not militant jihadis or illegal immigrants.

By not impeaching Obama our nationalist apathy will legally aid and abet our cultural death.

DEMOCRATS HATE LITTLE BABIES

Democrats: You don't protect babies--the most innocent and vulnerable of all? Get ready to fall.

People lined up to adopt these babies--not abort--but this dems in blood lust will always thwart.

They make fun of women--look what they do to Hillary Clinton. But of course she deserves it: vermin.

Deny climate change, lose gun rights! Are you kidding--while shutting down our lights?

In a nation who doesn't protect babies, why would they care that Bill Clinton raped so many ladies?

What's he gonna do to us next? For eight years we were under daily torture with the Obama hex.

Obama was taking over through the expansion of bureaucracies then making congress fall in with out mercy.

PRETENTIOUS SLOBS

The impeachment committee found 44 criminal charges against Obama. Such was our daily trauma!

He's compelled to target us because we're weak by putting up with him and obeying such freaks.

TREASON GOES UNPUNISHED

Those who know about the crime of treason and do nothing are as guilty as the one.

The problem with American Individualism is we don't community-organize like liberals, progressives and pres.

The traitor has already targeted you as his enemy. Now man up and fight back against tyranny!

There are 200 countries in the world and only 6 can defend themselves. Guns make us individuals.

America is an anti-rape culture. In history our women slapped faces with the slightest disrespect, for sure.

Thank you God for raising up Donald Trump so he can save the country after so much treason/treachery.

I'm done. As the Titanic goes down (though Trump could turn it all around) I choose being renowned.

America's beautiful but won't be when the grid goes down--toilets unflushed, trash not picked up: no fun.

Conservatives are individuals so the problem is: we don't community-organize like dems or ISIS.

We were so scared we didn't know what to do. Our leader told us all was great but we knew, not true.

Fascism: merger of government and corporate. It means tyranny which is destructive and morbid.

PRETENTIOUS SLOBS

Patriots are persecuted and if we don't stop it it'll spread like cancer but Trump is the answer.

TYRANNIES: TAXES, FINES AND FEES

Taxes, fines and fees: that's the mark of Tyrannies and it all starts by giving stuff away for free.

Fighting for liberty is the animating contest bringing you to your best: Handsome/pretty with zest.

You gotta tell your sexual history to enter colleges now. Like a cult of perversity of Satan or Mao.

We already know he's the worst guy there ever was, no need to know the rest. We're scared/depressed.

The good leader unites everyone while the bad leader divides them--he's always triggering em, amen?

Fox has failed. They're increasingly anti-Trump and anything good and decent they've derailed.

The career criminal Hillary Clinton has fallen like a rock. Praise God we're rid of hideous double-talk.

At first they all shun patriots but later when it's accepted and costs nothing they'll all join us/be buddies.

Tolerance is the oldest American principal, but not for that--unless you're a pervert or imbecile.

They're so wrong and we're so right this revolution of ideas will be quick like a thief in the night.

The liberal agenda: Safe space Orwellian social justice warrior new world order hell in America.

In the sixties hippies were called "loving" but now they're in power and it's tyranny (crushing).

PRETENTIOUS SLOBS

PEDOPHILES WANT RIGHTS TOO

It's a liberal worldview seeing all humans as deserving of rights even the most perverse: yikes!

MAPS: Minor Attracted Persons (euphemism for pedophiles)

Banned from twitter for right-wing views yet they're allowed to advocate pedophilia in youtube videos.

Pedophiles: Atheists disbelieving in good vs. evil so liberals never see them as truly bad people.

Anyone buying the leftist line--even one little slogan--will be less than he is and not well-spoken.

The Age of Cowardice is coming to an end just as the Age of Men is beginning to return, amen.

Tyrants say anyone trying to promote liberty is a "terrorist" and it's this us patriots must resist.

When liberals hear "Nazi" they think "right wing". But Hitler was a liberal socialist vegan who didn't drink.

Through Donald we can return from the brink. If you can't see the state we're in you need a shrink.

The message was: "don't mess with us". This was very serious as we faced terrible tyranny in the U.S.

The liberal publisher said "If we took out all the offensive parts there wouldn't be a book left"--complement.

The world's been waiting for a leader who speaks from the heart not phony teleprompters, for a start.

FEMINISTS LOVE BIG GOVERNMENT

Dumb females love to rely on government. It's like their daddy since they've degraded real men.

PRETENTIOUS SLOBS

Instead of modest sweet little ladies, women have become monsters listening to feminists so shady.

He was fomenting race wars, can't you see that? A true leader is a unifier not a dirty divisive rat.

"Trumpism": Expression of legitimate anger over American events and the belief only Trump can solve it.

Liberals have nothing to say, they're empty. It's all talking points, party lines and whatever's trendy.

The 5-4 SCOTUS majority was the only check on the left's gov expansion to take all of our property.

From London to New York people's heads are down, terrified. That's what happens with lost pride.

America: This leader has beat us up daily and many feel chagrin. You must feel big and proud again.

Revitalization Movements led by one with charisma bring sudden reversals-- prosperity in America!

God help us, the country's been betrayed! But we can still come back if enough of us prayed.

Adapting to liberal culture brings grossness. A grossification of America has occurred, replacing greatness.

TYRANTS AND PROCRASTINATORS

They get upset all day about things that don't matter. That's the left and feminists lost in chatter.

It's never been so urgent for men to find their male side (the animus) by rising up (despite feminists).

People are waking up in huge numbers! Thank you God for opening minds previously encumbered.

PRETENTIOUS SLOBS

Tho' enthused at first the flame dies and he goes slow, gets lazy, doesn't know, has no empathy for y'all.

Enthused at first then they flake out. Happy to promise/plan then becomes cold, zombie, a different man.

No staying power, weak foundation, limp handshake, vacillates--that's the immature man/THIRD RATE.

He always thinks he can do it, explosive acceptance--but then distracted by whatever catches his glance.

If they know how important it is to you that's precisely when they'll withdraw/withhold giving it.

Progressives caught in a "purity spiral" of demanding more and more strict adherence to their bull.

LASCIVIOUS LIBERALISM

There is relentless dishonesty in the very people paid highly to inform us.

Why think you're helping the kids who are grandstanding and you're going along with their manipulation?

How are university professors helping, allowing attention-getting narcissistic undergrads taking over class?

"Emancipatory Politics" is hexed as it "repairs" discriminated groups and puts down dominant whites.

Everyone does it, it's always been that way, you have your sins too. That's the three con jobs for you.

Liberals are calling names while conservatives make arguments--no connection so be done with em.

The worst thing you can do is tell mentally ill liberals that they're brilliant, entitled and deceived.

PRETENTIOUS SLOBS

You think they're all nice? This isn't the fifties--these are the latter days and it's scary as God repays.

SOAPS LURE WOMEN INTO NARRATIVE

Soaps: They wanna lure us in with a love story of conflict, then slip in pure debauchery and the deviant.

People are sick and getting sicker as they all degenerate together. Seen thru the eyes of God it's a horror.

God is purity, order, goodness. Not this mess coming over the human race creating such nastiness.

TV has a moral responsibility because people copy everything they see unless firmly grounded in morality.

The world cannot hate you but it hates Me because I testify of it that its works are evil. John 6: 7:7

Don't argue with people on the other side. Save yourself a lot of energy: avoid leftists and the snide.

I'm not speaking again, they're too mean. They have no knowledge, they wanna get back, they are fiends.

When will everyone get past the peer pressure and admit it is true?

I see y'all falling away into occult, false teachings and debauchery. This shows weakness/lack of mastery.

Totally dangerous: We want to be liked more than telling the truth.

THEIR ONLY RECOGNITION IS VICTIM-VALIDATION

The young liberals don't do great things for recognition but tend to fall into victimhood for validation.

Obloquy: Widespread censure or abuse; disgrace resulting from this.

In this generation, anonymity is safety.

PRETENTIOUS SLOBS

Nazis were socialists, the KKK were democrats and the white man freed the slaves.

Secret societies like Masons lowers Christ in the scheme of things or puts Him equal with other gods.

"Those who stand for nothing will fall for anything". That is so true and I saw that in many friends I knew.

Or if they say "it's always been that way", normalizing perversion--hit the road/avoid destruction.

Everyone does it, it's always been that way, you have your sins too: Normalizing sin by liberal friends of you.

They've been so cut off from their destiny they're little barbarians, shallow roots adapting to ruffians.

If you don't go along with them they censure you, de-platform you and then go after your banking.

There is no end to perversion until Jesus puts an end to it. it's depthless, fathomless, bottomless.

You're riding a wave cuz that's the current narrative but wait till things change--you'll face what you did.

Let God take care of things, it'll be much worse for your enemies. Vengeance is His, the best--believe me.

Comedians can't tell unapproved jokes, scientists must abandon politically unpopular research.

Wherever democracy is allowed the progressive globalist left is doomed. They know that, terrified too.

THE DEAD VOTE DEMOCRAT, LITERALLY

The dead vote democrat.

PRETENTIOUS SLOBS

I too was entrenched in the dirty generation and came back to reality taking the values of grandma and God.

American-hating forces have come out of the woodwork to stop the recovery--wanting us down, not up.

Stop telling our wonderful president to "tone it down". He'll lose his great personality: why he won.

Don't you dare tone it down President Trump! We love your sass/you have class, please keep it up!

The left says: "I want to feel good about myself so I'll MAKE them do something generous on my behalf."

Dear Mr. Trump: Please do not tone down your speech, be more harsh, please!

The irony of the left: They tell us what we're seeing with our own eyes doesn't exist so why are we pist?

Nazis killed 150+ million people and they call us Nazis? What an insult, don't let em do this, it's crazy.

Trump: Beautiful deals with democrats or warlike retaliation for probes? You choose: he loves or scolds.

Truth mixed with error is still error. The problem is mixture.

Antifa's home invasion will make Tucker more popular than ever as the Streisand effect takes over.

I will never watch FOX again except for Tucker, Hannity and Ingraham--the others have sold out, friends.

THE SAVIOR OF AMERICA

Trump has done more this country than ever in history and you ingrates hate him still, hot coals of treachery.

Trump and cronies have it all in a bag. Thousands are going to prison and we'll recall you arrogant cads.

PRETENTIOUS SLOBS

If you're into occult--a Christian believing in reincarnation, a nut--you should be afraid of hell and repent.

When things finally turn around and the criminals are in jail we'll recall how you flaked out and failed.

After 8 years of the trauma of Obama, that's it--we're at our end! Pray for clarity and perseverance friends.

When Facebook isn't banning you they're blocking your likes! You don't know who loves you/who hates.

You don't have to explain cuz if you explain you put yourself on their level, way down with the devil.

The center left is collapsing as it's cut to half or less. People want tradition back cuz this means happiness.

Progressive underground is anti-tradition and based on the 60's sexual liberation movement.

JUST DESTROY THE OLD ORDER

It's the total destruction of the Old Order based on Christianity and the moral absolutes implied.

It's the ushering in of an occult new age. A socialistic kingdom of conformity to an illusion of falsehoods.

It's a Pantheistic New World Order on earth and it's fancy illusions combined with fascistic communism.

FOX: Anti-Trump stuff ticked me off but now it's ramped up: Tucker and Hannity face a hostile environment.

Apparently blacks will love you if you're a lying corrupt person giving them free stuff as evil is called "good".

Reason for mass riots of young men across the world: it's our fault for not giving opportunities/more?

PRETENTIOUS SLOBS

My best advice is: let Trump do his job. For unobstructed that's his genius, didn't you know?

At least Mussolini made the trains run on time but De Blasio makes nothing run on time. Michael Savage

HAVE FUN EXPOSING PEOPLE!

Yes I do have fun exposing these people, to reveal how vacuous and moronic they really are.

Thank God for our president, it's our blessed destiny to experience it but sure feels like living on the edge.

DROP EM if they say "everyone does it" or "you have your sins too".

It's a hostile invasion of young men fighting age!

Low IQ cultures: trash, violence.   High IQ cultures: clean order and refinement.

21st Century warfare is using millions of people as political weapons.

Import the third world, become the third world--simple as that.

Everything we are--our very selves--will be lost if we turn the country over to people who are not us!

Nationalism: Pride in neat clean streets, happiness. Globalism: Trash everywhere/mean creeps.

Yes diversity is nice--music and food--but that's as long as they stay unique, not globalist pawns/freaks.

What is a traitor? One who prefers outsiders!

Nationalism is the opposite to patriotism? Why are they listed as synonyms, Mr. Macron?

Diversity means: less white people.

PRETENTIOUS SLOBS

Low IQ pops: Trashy and violent. High IQ pops: Pristine cities and villages, respectful and decent.

Macron took a WWI memorial event as his chance to take a swipe at Trump's vision (anti-global) nationalism.

MEMORIALS OF PAST ARE USED TO BASH

WWI Memorial to the millions of men who died for nationalism against which Macron grandstands?

Americans will never knowingly adopt socialism but through liberalism will accept it all. Norman Thomas

We fight to defend our home/bill of rights--anything else is a racket and organized crime. Smedley Butler

Armies, debts/taxes are the instruments bringing the many under the domination of the few. James Madison

When the whole world lives in your country nothing survives. Mixing means ALL traditions worn away.

The native people of a land should never be made a minority within it. Shoot me, I must be a bigot.

Higher IQs make them harder to deceive, keep in captivity or control. That's the west when we were bold.

Citizens of the west are historically the hardest to rule over or oppress--we have the right to self-defense.

SHARIA is brutality we hate (and gives us nightmares at night) because we believe in human rights.

We don't care about tweets we just want the wall, that's all.

Affluent liberals in power never think about this travesty. They're in white gated communities neat/orderly.

PRETENTIOUS SLOBS

The higher the IQ the more gentle/genteel, the lower the more rapacious, animalistic and unempathic.

IT'S WHITE REPLACEMENT

This isn't about replacing us, oh no. This is about helping people who are less fortunate/living low.

You went through that cuz you hadn't learned boundaries. Without that the world flows in, evil cronies.

Attitude of mine: I don't wear a gun cuz I hate the people outside but because I love the people inside.

Tell the nutty: Baptized globalism (open borders and amnesty) is worlds apart from biblical Christianity.

Southern Border: It's always a serious thing when the military's called in: very good or very bad.

If music and drama is to satisfy everyone it won't satisfy anyone.

Merkel and Mae care only for outsiders, not insiders--and that is mental illness in the human herd, traitors.

UK: Paying em all to leave would be a helluva lot cheaper than allowing em to stay so save England, ok?

Pay em to get rid of em--the only answer for Londonstan and the rest of em--or we're dead, the white man.

Tolerance, openness and diversity now sends England back to the 7th century.

You know it all anyway, we're going to hell. That's surrounded by strangers who don't share our values.

Soros wants Israel removed saying it doesn't have a right to exist and if you criticize this you're anti-semitic.

Border Hassle: If you throw rocks it'll be treated as if it was a rifle! Pres. Trump

PRETENTIOUS SLOBS

Elites are collapsing the third world so they can take over with tyranny. Everyone poor, the top bossy.

Curious funding streams.

There are people who want to take countries we love to hell in a handcart with no breaks. Katie Hopkins

THE RIGHT TO DIS-ASSOCIATION

It doesn't matter if we're poor, in shambles, invaded in our own homes because we're "culturally enriched".

Eastern Europeans have maintained the "tragic sense of life" and won't let them in but we've forgotten.

Why welcome people who don't share our values? Can you tell me this, if it destroys me and you?

Diversity is the religion of our time. It's like "we are one" which is a lie while destroying our very lives.

The EU was a Nazi plan--paradise of the future. It's not Trump who is nazi it is Macron, tyrant for hire.

I'm aware of the cosmic vision and it's communism. I was taken in too, long ago while I was still fishin'

The end of May and Merkel is here, symbolizing the stupidity of emotional women causing ruin/fear.

The glories of multiculturalism is sad illusion when in fact it's ghettos of POCs who hate each other.

Rights of Muslim communities not to be offended are greater than our rights to free speech. Katie Hopkins

500 million more: Why we hate Macron (toxic weasel) even more than Merkel and May, angels of treason.

PRETENTIOUS SLOBS

To the new age, "universal values" means debauchery, loss of freedom and privacy, invasion by nasty.

Free market capitalism has been the greatest wealth-creating engine in the history of the world.

CAPITALISM BRINGS DOWN POVERTY

World poverty has gone down from 70% to 10% not from socialism but from free-market capitalism.

No one EVER flees free market capitalism to go back to socialism. Would they go back to Venezuela?

Paris looks more like a bazaar for illegal migrants. Paris trip advisor review

They care more about the extinction of the mold beetle than white people.

Economic migrants become a client group the state controls. Despite murder and rape it's power ya know.

Leaked Soros docs confirm migrant crisis a tool of "global governance". Good grief wake up, liberal dunces.

Swedish rape stats show 80% are foreign born.

The elites push migrant policies where they're not bearing the brunt of the resulting catastrophes.

The current mode is collective punishment which is the opposite to justice.

Macron agrees Europe needs 200 MILLION migrants in the next 30 years, he's the Kalergi Plan enforcer.

We don't want em here cuz we know MAL-ADAPTATION to insane or loose environments is our.

Tip for hot Paris trip: don't step in the shit.

To repeat. Macron: In the next 30 years 200 MILLION MORE are coming but we have Big Daddy.

PRETENTIOUS SLOBS

Once western culture becomes the minority view you won't have free speech or women's rights ever again.

WEALTHY RACE HUSTLERS

How do race hustlers get power and wealth? By yelling "racist" that's how.

To find out who rules over you find out who you're not allowed to criticize.

With time the only thing worth talking about can't be talked about.

Signs of radically changed demography: Bags of shit on Frisco sidewalks, bags of body parts in NYC, yuk.

Whites, please have babies. We don't like--we abhor--these cruel brutal cultures with different realities.

They want us all brown, period. One big bag of it easily malleable and accepting of tyranny/used to it.

These people lack empathy and have totally different values when it comes to dear animals/go to hell!

When it comes to animals even the tender mercies of the wicked are cruel.

They love and enjoy working in meat packing industries. Have you ever wondered why, softies?

While flooded with disparate cultures making us sick all we can do is fence up and live our own trip.

They change the four olds: Old ideas, old culture, old customs and old habits but we don't want this.

We console ourselves in this terrible period by pretending it's not going on.

Thomas Jefferson's version of fake news: the "lies of the day"

Because of Trump, veterans are the new elites. Feminists with comfy existence should just shut up, the creeps.

PRETENTIOUS SLOBS

Photos make us vulnerable since they're so into looks/critical and we're more into the spiritual (invisible).

MISERY CAMARADERIE

It's phony, scary, weird, fake happy, so boring everyone's smiling, say nothing misery camaraderie.

What are they laughing about? It's a phony social glue or veneer smoothing reality with other fakers.

It's always grit on my nerves, hysterical laughing like the cackling of thorns hiding such darkness, forlorned.

Liberalism is a mental illness and if you have to adapt to it (like boss or spouse) you become crazy.

The fake virtue signaling left are always moralizing yet stand for the lowest evils and debaucheries.

THE DIET OF FREEDOM!

Start the diet of freedom having banished all distractions from your purpose-work without these burdens.

God's wisdom is all you need to transcend your weird world. Fools hate knowledge, prepare for scorn.

The world's wisdom and God's are opposites, so learn to savor sweet saintly solitude and like me, LOVE IT.

Well you've seen the light and now you have no friends! Don't fret just get to know God as life mends.

You're in training--God knows your future. Jealousy brings anger: they made you feel small/you were in danger.

They wanted power over you to compensate their lowness in comparison, as witchcraft takes over nation.

DISCOVERIES DON'T TELL THEY TRIGGER

PRETENTIOUS SLOBS

A discovery doesn't tell, it triggers--the reader sees unconscious analogies in self and it's sudden/rigorous.

It's not like a treatise or journal article but an art piece that opens up the mind's portals and it's wonderful.

It takes GUTS to do this: not write boring journal articles for approval but poetry for neurosis-removal.

Academia is boring and who are they kidding? They tweak the stats to confirm whatever they're thinking.

They get grants for their viewpoint so will they modify it when wrong? I doubt it, they're the herd/the throng.

GENIUS IS HELD DOWN BY *PEOPLE*

Genius is held down by people, habit and food. He's stigmatized for differences and held down by groups.

Genius is blocked by groups and then by his own addictions to avoid anxiety from persecution and it sux.

If persecuted genius eats wrong he's held down by ugly weight on top of hate and If he drinks, bad fate.

As body gets tiny, mind explodes to higher dimensions as the temporal lobe opens to Einstein's ETERNITY.

Look forward with glee. Notice I'm not posting politics, I've given up on that-- just my work and Thee.

Morbid cultural fears about aging are opposite to the truth. Never forget all popular notions are false!

The horrible actors in my past wrote these ten books--gotta remember that or resentment makes me a kook.

Yes the herd keeps you down but past memories (ouch) are the little anchors keeping you there.

PRETENTIOUS SLOBS

TRANSCEND HIX POLITIX

He overwhelmed Biden and did it HIS way. He was called "gross" but he didn't care, his country came first.

It worked, he dominated. Far worse groundless insults came from Biden to our Pres.--like "SHUT UP"

Thoughts about the foe keeps you a victim. Fame is flying above it all and not staying hooked/forget em.

The actors in my life (teaching me what not to be) were just a sample of how they all are so I thank Thee.

In your eighties you begin to maximize mental powers for as physical wanes the mystical genius takes over.

I can be in a quandary then I pray and suddenly God clears is all up. It's always so genius, so great/on top.

You come to a point where even you can't mess up your success. It's in the works/taken years not months.

It's all done and recognizable from afar--you're just putting last minute details in place, infinitesimal, a trace.

We're taught to conform to the same mold: the standard one in society and it can be Procrustean/deadly.

PROCRUSTEAN CONFORMITY

Procrusteas was a giant who stretched or amputated captives to fit his iron bed: split from self, dead.

Losing self is a homesick life making us seek out others more, losing self more--succeed by going SOLO.

Solo is with God--separate is sanctified, holy. People-adaptation is a life of missed miracles/lost opportunity.

PRETENTIOUS SLOBS

Miracles happening every second but you're lost in loony logorrhea: word salad, silliness and trivia.

If you love people help em transcend blocks to creativity in dense herds and become their True Self.

BE A SHINING EXEMPLAR

Be a shining light/exemplar to the race. Don't work to confirm their boring narrative just erase.

Having transcended blocks you become cosmic: influenced not by people but by God's creative spirit.

People will only hold you down. Some will help but they're so rare it isn't even worth checking out.

Be a shining light/exemplar to the race. Don't work to confirm their boring narrative just erase.

Man is an adaptive animal--he adapts to his environment. When it's sick he's sick, a life of frenetic stress.

Self-image is relational so when you grow up they face what they did to you as a screw up.

When I forgave my mother long dead I stopped mimicking her, an unconscious device instead.

SOCIAL HYPNOTISM

He went away suddenly when I was rejected by the group. Social acceptance was everything to him, stupid.

From the first day of kindergarden i went from happy child to miserable and feeling hated/forgotten.

Before conversion life is chaotic and dark made dense from people, habit or food obstructions.

PRETENTIOUS SLOBS

People are like animals in their group behavior--mimicking and following each other like a flock of birds.

People can hold you down as maintaining the system--the status quo--- becomes the glue of groups.

Since identity is relational the system must keep the parts in their place to maintain the status quo.

Since identity is relational they destroy others to maintain it: keep each other down like crabs in a bucket.

Sick family systems will keep the patient down and sabotage recovery for the sake of their own identity.

BAD HABITS MAINTAIN BAD MEMORIES

Bad habits maintain bad memories which trigger the craving to sin, reinforcing the bad memory again.

To mature to genius success, wipe the past clean then a clean slate each day so old cycles are passe.

A temptation habitually denied will cease to exist but will gain stronger hold each time we give in, promise.

To attract success the Creative Act must be complete. It's just a few more days so don't get complacent please.

Once completion has occurred it's an instant magnet to world success as it all opens up for the genius.

Genius conflicts with petty forces pulling him down to something they can understand/must be overcome.

Can the genius overcome these resistances, rise up in spite of them and make his amazing new dent?

Moral purity overcomes resistance but sin weakens so sudden success is followed by overnight fall.

PRETENTIOUS SLOBS

Sin creates arrogance which always precedes downfall.

The bible's clear on the evil of latter days: men as lovers of self/money, arrogant malicious gossipers.

Now men are without self-control, brutal and vicious haters of good, treacherous, reckless, conceited.

Men steeped in religion but unholy, ever learning but never coming to the truth-- scapegoating me and you.

PRIMITIVE GENIUS HAS MUCH TO OVERCOME

Primitive genius has much to overcome as his radical differences prevent adaptation to dense scum.

High-tech progress veils severe degeneration in mind, spirit, body, family, and the knit of society.

Video games are meaningless life. Quit, gain strength, get smart, become a leader and escape strife.

Genius is a rose hitting a hard wall: most give up or die through self-destructive addictions to avoid anxiety.

Through knowledge he gains power over the human herd maintaining cohesion by destroying differences.

Genius is champion standing out in a sea of sharks, reflecting God's blueprint not minds of men so dark.

The mind of God transcends culture and silly human fashions--of thoughts, morality and customs.

You cannot be saved and into black magic too--reincarnation, necromancy, occult fantasies--can you?

Genius deals with these times by becoming sensitive to the works of God: nature, seasons, love.

PRETENTIOUS SLOBS

Becoming Godly brings awareness of the futility of the ungodly: failing, vanity, carnality and misery.

Everything is energy and if open we sing, dance and soar. Dormant genius awakes, making new dents in the world.

The clear attracts success against overwhelming odds. He has freedom from obstruction and God.

He knows how people hold him down/how bad habits degrade so in purity focuses on work each day.

FORGET BLAME IF *YOU* LET EM IN!

Her influence was bad though I'm to blame cuz I didn't discern. It's just that she was in my life so I deferred.

Grow up and hot coals on their head. God doesn't have to punish them, it's relational identity instead.

Cosmic man does nothing. Clarity puts him in synchronicity of magic coincidence as he attracts.

In peace he has total power. Having emptied himself of all obstructions he's now man of the hour.

He's an irresistible magnet to good attractions while repelling all-bad. Effortless grace cuz God's his Dad.

Rid of obstructions he rules by attraction--a paradigm shift to energy has one general formula, exaction.

My only claim to fame is I love God and did the work. Take your time finishing/make it perfect.

Deliberately stop work at the end. Let it be something you just wanna do, an inertia towards completion.

GLOBAL BULLIES

PRETENTIOUS SLOBS

Globalists are formulaic and they're making their move. Crashed borders must be stopped, I behoove!

Muslims are God to the left because they have the same enemy: the West.

Corporate international elite works with authoritarian regimes to bring in cashless society and grief.

What UN has planned for us: Smash us together violently then claim the spoils when the dust settles.

Many Americans want to sacrifice freedom so they can virtue signal to the rest of us and not be "racist".

Order from chaos is precisely what the globalists want and we see it in these borders overrun.

The first border invasion was just a test, a probe. They're planning a much bigger one now ya know.

Giant dumbed down populations are being marched into the west to bankrupt our social safety net.

Once the west is collapsed it'll be a mass of poor people controlled by vicious waiting technocrats.

Trump's the real deal, he did what he said he'd do--that's why the power structure wants him moved.

Any hint of disapproval is now a hate crime in the U.K.

YELLOW JACKETS ARE ABOUT INVASION

It's finally admitted France's yellow jacket riots are not just about gas but immigrant floods/a mess.

Western European is giving up its culture, comfort and space to people who see Europe as nothing but prey.

Genocide by substitution is the crime against humanity in the 21st century.

PRETENTIOUS SLOBS

If trust is broken in one place restrictions are imposed everywhere: that's like China I declare.

Reject Totalitarian Replacism or die cuz you won't survive.

Since the Russian collusion was proven an illusion when to the trials begin for treason? Donald J. Trump

Never forget, the demonrats are for abortion up to birth and beyond--infanticide. They are WRETCHED.

Who cares about Trump's taxes? He doesn't take a salary, what else can he do to prove his sincerity?

The only real emergency is the tyranny emerging. Owen Shroyer

DAILY: DATES, SPUDS/RICE, MUSE/SLEEP

It's the contrast of starch/salt vs. sugar/succulent. That's the balance and I'm wondering if it's the apex.

I prefer a smoothie diet where I don't have to deal with acid reflux, over-fullness or sleepiness.

I like popcorn too, it's near-zero glycation like white rice/sugar and a tasty treat in the afternoon.

When you get as food-apathetic as I have the smoothie's the biggest vitamineral meal, the way it is.

When you eat something then choke in your sleep it's a warning signal. Eat early, rest safe/stay humble.

When you get as food-apathetic as me the smoothie's the biggest vitamineral meal savored early.

Gut or tooth pain--which is worse? It's the kind that makes you lie down and pray God ends this curse.

A day comes when you take your health very seriously. No more fooling around it's too darn excruciating.

PRETENTIOUS SLOBS

I can't put away a bag of Cheetos like I did back in the day. It's indigestive catastrophe/could be lethal, ok?

As MacDougal said we HEAL totally and only by the cessation of self-poisoning: truth simply.

EVERYTHING'S COVERED IN FAT/SOY

Everything's covered in FAT & SOY. That's why the human race has corrupted/ the physical distorted--oh boy.

Why do they want us fat, angry, bloated and distorted? Cuz in our self-disgust our destiny's aborted.

As he made clear it's not just fruit it's starch too and that's the palatable factor making it do-able.

I need sweet/succulent balanced with starchy/salty--without this balance it's no good the next day.

Breakfast: dates are good. Lunch: starch/rice is good. Dinner: juice or skip it, don't wanna choke on it.

Dates, rice, fast. As an elder I'm not into eating just thinking/ruminating so this is how I do it.

Dates kill cancer. Ok fine now eat eight dates for breakfast everyday and you have that covered.

It's about getting thru the day, fueling the tank, getting the job done so you can find your destiny.

This century's fruitarians made too big a deal of eating, eating, eating! Avoid fruitarian gluttony/be saintly.

To avoid any more humiliating failures I had to go 100%. For hypersensitives that's the way it is.

Fruitarianism is to be a spiritual trip and tyrannical forcefeeding of 3 grand calories goes against this.

PRETENTIOUS SLOBS

LADYLIKE DATES NOT 1000 BANANAS

What could be more ladylike than a couple dates on the sly not smacking, slurping/constant fruit eating.

It's not that I'm preparing for death but jettisoning all superfluity for the final hurrah.

We have "turgid" thoughts when fecal matter fills the cells and that's depression, pessimism, giving up.

Not only am I physically incapable of eating that much fruit, I'm mentally blocked too--I just wanna mind-cruise!

Fruitarianism is an esoteric life not a frenetic one. Altho' one gets busy as the creative becomes fun.

I got so tired of them saying to "eat, eat, eat". We all know the benefits of fasting so this is false belief.

Can't believe how we were told to eat coconut in all it's forms yet here it's one of the highest glicators.

If you didn't eat enough fruit they'd react/drop you from the group. Think back--you know it too.

I'm gaining faith in DATES. I prognosticate a complete healing of the gut from burping/acid reflux.

AUTHOR'S LAST WORDS

The possibilities are endless if you think like this. Just wait, you'll be discovered in fastarian bliss.

Stop remorsing over the dead past when you soaked sin up like a sponge. You were just a sensitive, that's all.

We all swam in muddy waters, it got more mud on you than the others cuz sensitives are spongy fellers.

PRETENTIOUS SLOBS

I became worst of the lot cuz I needed more attention and that was how to get it--thats what I thought.

MUST GO 100% OR FORGET IT

To avoid any more humiliating failures I had to go 100%. For hypersensitives that's the way it is.

Don't tell me, I know the etiology of bad habits. But the superior man has control over things like that.

I contracted you for a job and now you're giving me lessons I never asked for. Stay specific, watch over.

Continually talking about your past shows you haven't resolved it yet by relying on the paid ransom.

Thus concludes a manual/writing from the left brain. I'm solidly on the right now: music w/out refrain.

You think all this is about you but I NEVER indicated who it was about tho' it pertains to more than a few.

When someone'comes off like a god when he's a mere mortal who sins like the rest of us, flawed.

I don't like interviews cuz they're not perfect like the Creative Act where each frame's checked.

The reason no one can live with me even in houses separately is cuz I want solitude you see.

Best advice of the year: Stop saying you're a content creator and just create content sir.

You must relax to get the gems looking back. Many of em hurt, you need to apologize sometimes: fact.

Though things look bleak we are told not to fear so look up for your salvation/joy is near.

PRETENTIOUS SLOBS

Act too soon, be a fool forever. Make sure things are right before pulling the trigger.

One party rule in one year destroying a nation: that's what we're watching and it's mostly women.

Pet shelters are concentration camps. They come out neurotic as hell, what to do about this?

BEAUTY WITHOUT SURGERY

How to not need botox for forehead wrinkles or surgery for other infinite incidentals: FAST.

A cheerful heart is good medicine, but a crushed spirit dries up the bones. Proverbs 17:22

We start with rubbery bones but with years of stress and bad events we end up brittle: God come!

100 KAREN KELLOCK BOOKS

AFFINITY OR MISERY
AGELESS CORNUCOPIA
AMERICA AWAKE!
AMERICA'S DAFT ERA
ARTS OF PALEO FASTING
AUTOPHAGY ON CHEATERS
BACKSTABBING NEUROTICS
BETRAYAL TRAUMA
BOOMERS AND BROKENNESS
BOOT ON NECK
CHAMPION GUIDES
COMMIE NUTHOUSE
COMMIES
COMMUNIST SPIRIT
CONTAGION OF MADNESS
CONTAGIOUS MADNESS
CULTURE CLASH BASHED
DAFT LEFT
DAILY FASTARIAN
DAM RATS
DIVERSITY IS CRUELTY
E-RACE WHITE
EVIL FREAKS (Beyond Gross)
THE END OR A BEND?
FEMALE BULLIES AND FEMI-NAZIS
FEMALE CARNALITY
FEMALE DUMB DOWN
FEMALE POWER DRIVE
FEMINISM AND RUIN 1 & 2
FIX FOR MISFITS
FOOLS & TRAMPS
FREEDOM SPEAKING
FRENEMY ENABLER
FRENEMY LIAR
FRENEMY THIEF
FRENEMY TRAITOR
TRENEMY TYRANT
GENIUS IS HELD DOWN
GLOBALISLAM
GOD USES THE FLAWED
HAZE OF THE LATTER DAYS

THE HERD IN WORDS
HIX POLITIX
HOW THEY RUINED US
JUST SKIP DINNER
LE FEMME AND THE COMMUNIST SPIRIT
LIBERAL CHAOS & ROT
LIBERAL DOUBLETHINK
LIBERAL GALL 1 & 2
LIBERAL SHOVE-DOWNS
LOCK YOUR GATE
LOSERS and Femme Fatales
MANUAL FOR SUPERIOR MEN
MODERN ART FROM HELL
MOSTLY FAKE
NOTES TO CHAMPS 1 & 2
OVERCOME FRENEMIES
PC MAKES US CRAZY
PEOPLE ARE CRUEL
PEOPLE PROBLEMS 1 & 2
PERSECUTED GENIUIS
POLI-PSYCH MYSTERIES
PRETENTIOUS SLOBS
QUEEN BEE
RED NEW DEAL
RETURNING TO FIRST NATURE
SEASON OF TREASON
SEPARATE MEANS HOLY
SOCIAL HYPNOTISM
SOLITUDE SOLUTION
SUPERCILIOUS
THE SCHOOLS SCREWED EM UP
TOAD TO PRINCE
TRIALS CYCLES
TRUMP VS. GROUP
TRUST IN TRASH
THE TRUTH ABOUT PEOPLE
UNDERHEANDEDLY CLEVER
WALK TALL WITHIN WALLS
WE'RE NOT ALL ONE
WINNERS SKIP DINNER
WORK OR SMERK

KAREN KELLOCK PH.D.

M.S. Political Science, San Diego State. Ph.D. in Psychology, University of California Irvine. Postdoctoral: UCI School of Medicine, Dept. of Psychiatry [NIMH Grants]. Developed the Debris Theory of Disease, a theory of system pathology in 120 books and 22 textbooks for the general public. The theory has a general formula: All disease is obstruction, all recovery is elimination, all success is attraction. The three obstructions are people, habit and food. Remove obstruction and snap to your goals, waiting in the wings.